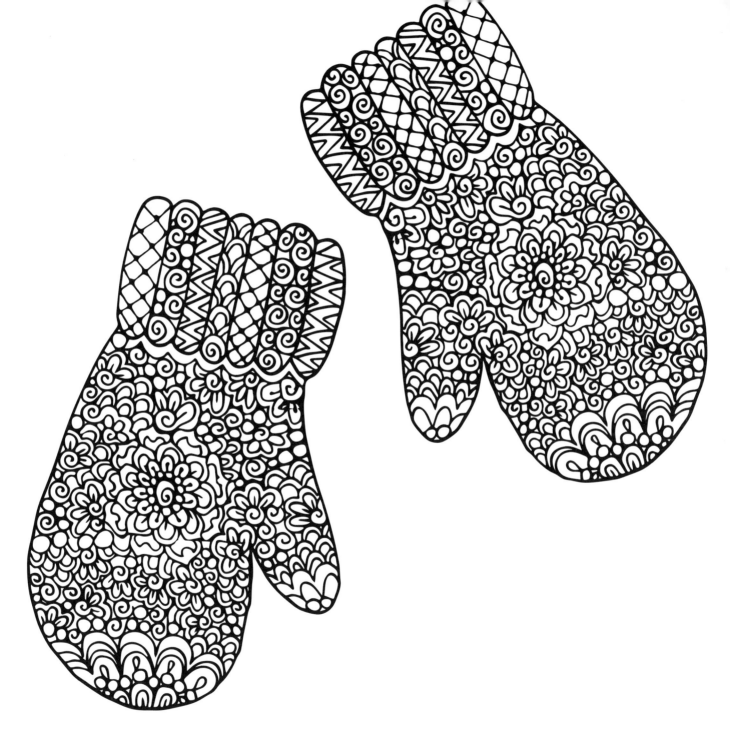

PLEASE LOOK FOR OTHER TITLES IN THE COLOR WITH MUSIC SERIES:

www.colorwithmusic.com

Published in 2016 by Newbourne Media LP, 1 Westmount Square, Suite 1100, Montreal, Quebec, Canada H3Z 2P9

Email: info@newbournemedia.com / Website: www.newbournemedia.com